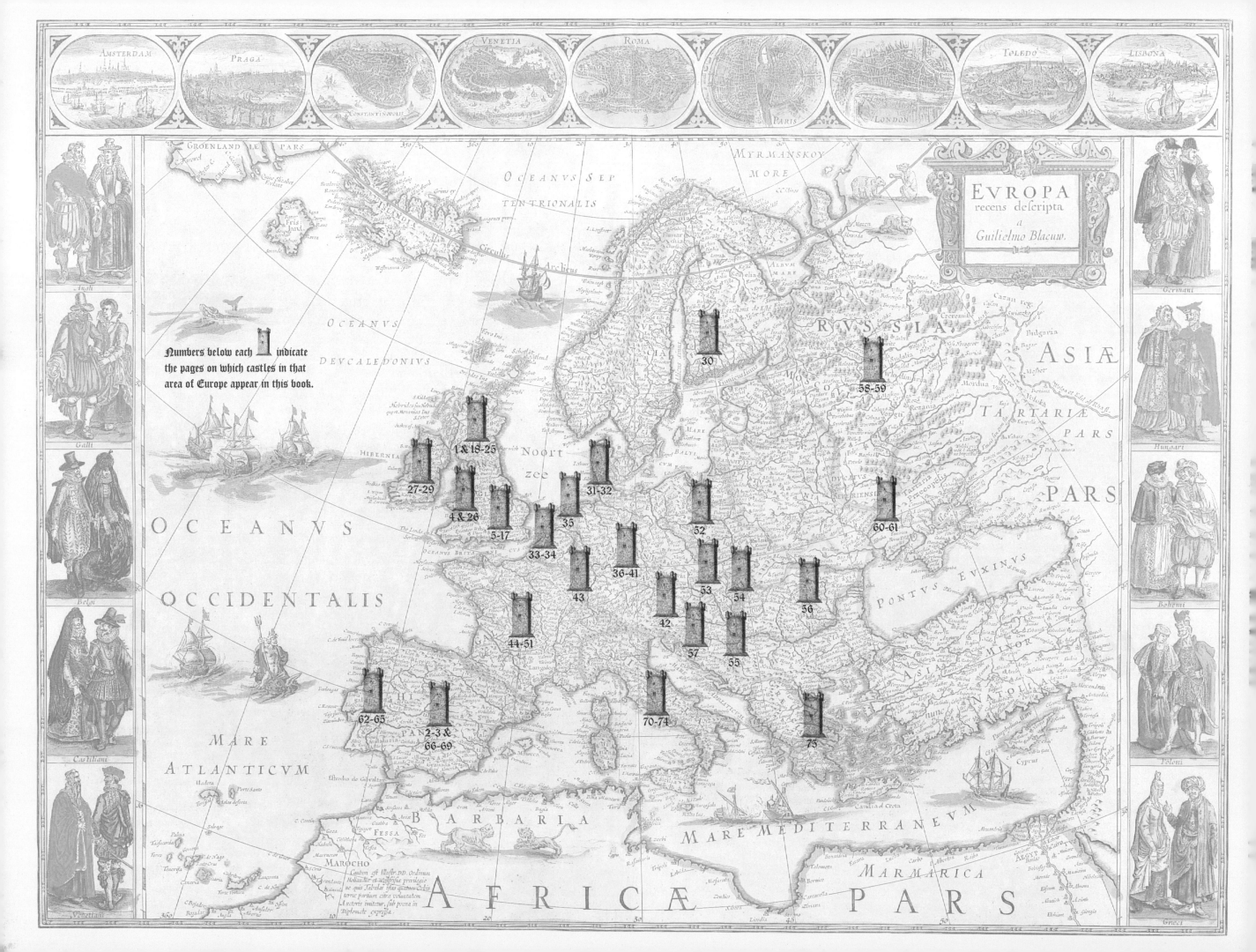

AMSTERDAM · PRAGA · VENETIA · ROMA · TOLEDO · LISBONA

CONSTANTINOPLE · PARIS · LONDON

EVROPA
recens descripta
a
Guilielmo Blaeuw.

Numbers below each ⌂ indicate the pages on which castles in that area of Europe appear in this book.

1 & 18-25

27-29

4 & 26

5-17

33-34

35

31-32

30

58-59

60-61

52

36-41

43

53

54

56

42

57

55

44-51

62-65

2-3 &
66-69

70-74

75

OCEANVS OCCIDENTALIS

MARE ATLANTICVM

AFRICÆ PARS

MARE MEDITERRANEVM

MARMARICA

Castles
Royal Homes and Fortresses of Europe

Castles

Royal Homes and Fortresses of Europe

PHOTO SELECTION AND TEXT

JOE GANNON

Castle Conwy (Conway),
in the town of Conwy, Aberconwy,
and Colwyn, north Wales.

Castles:
Royal Homes and Fortresses of Europe
Photo Selection and Text by Joe Gannon

For complete photographic credits please see page 80.

© 2008 by Mud Puddle Books, Inc.

Published by
Mud Puddle Books, Inc.
54 W. 21st Street
Suite 601
New York, NY 10010
info@mudpuddlebooks.com

ISBN: 978-1-60311-158-4

Printed in Thailand

Contents

Warwick Castle,
Warwickshire, England.

Bodiam Castle,
Sussex, England.

10

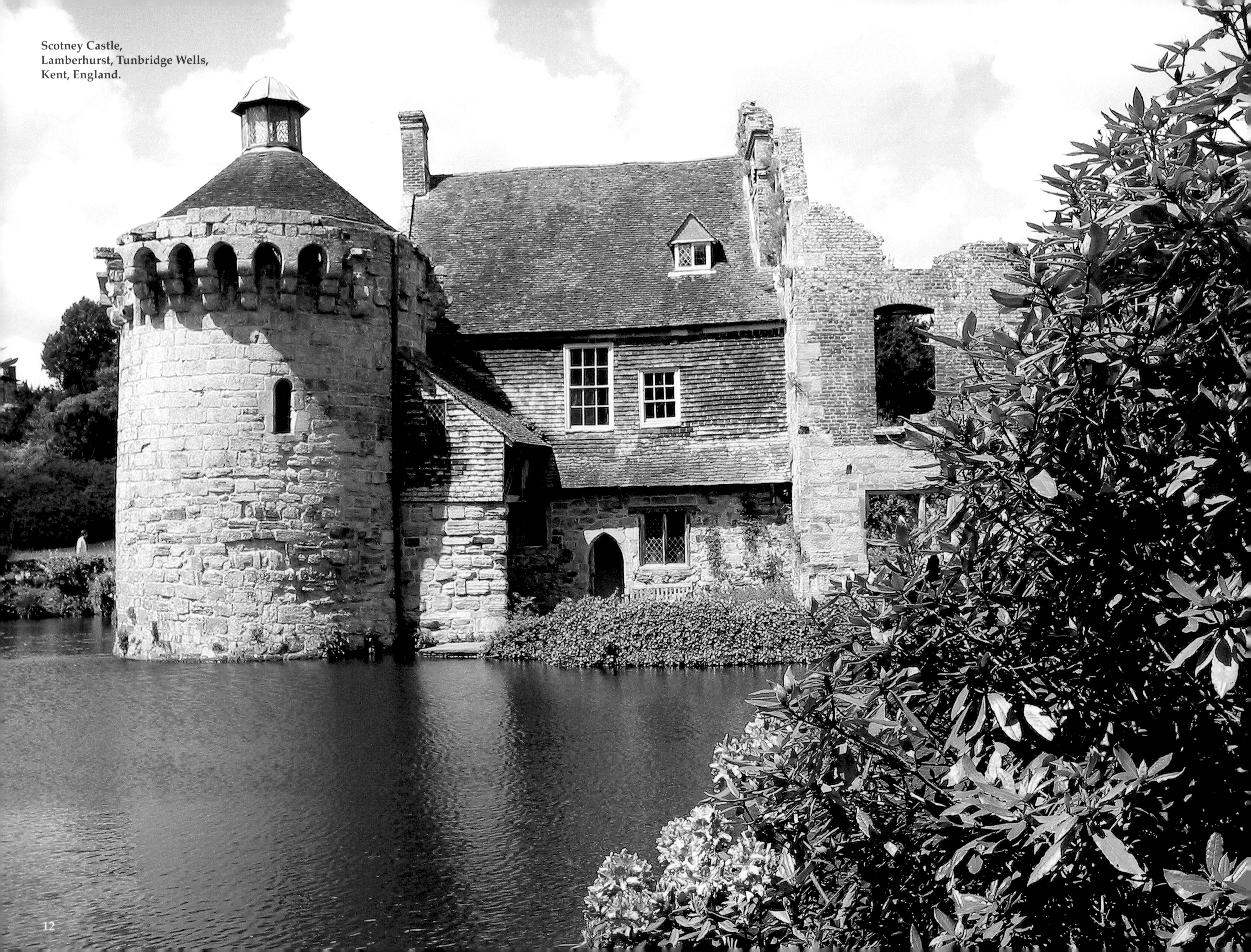

Scotney Castle,
Lamberhurst, Tunbridge Wells,
Kent, England.

The Tower of London,
London, England.

Hever Castle,
Kent, England.

Alnwick Castle,
Northumberland, England.

Leeds Castle,
Kent, England.

17

Dunrobin Castle,
Southerland, Scotland.

Balmoral Castle,
Aberdeenshire, Scotland.

Glamis Castle,
Angus, Scotland.

Palace of Holyroodhouse,
Edinburgh, Scotland.

Augustinian Abbey and gardens of the Palace.

Caerlaverock Castle,
Southeast of Dumfries, Scotland.

23

Lews Castle
Stornoway, Isle of Lewis,
Scotland.

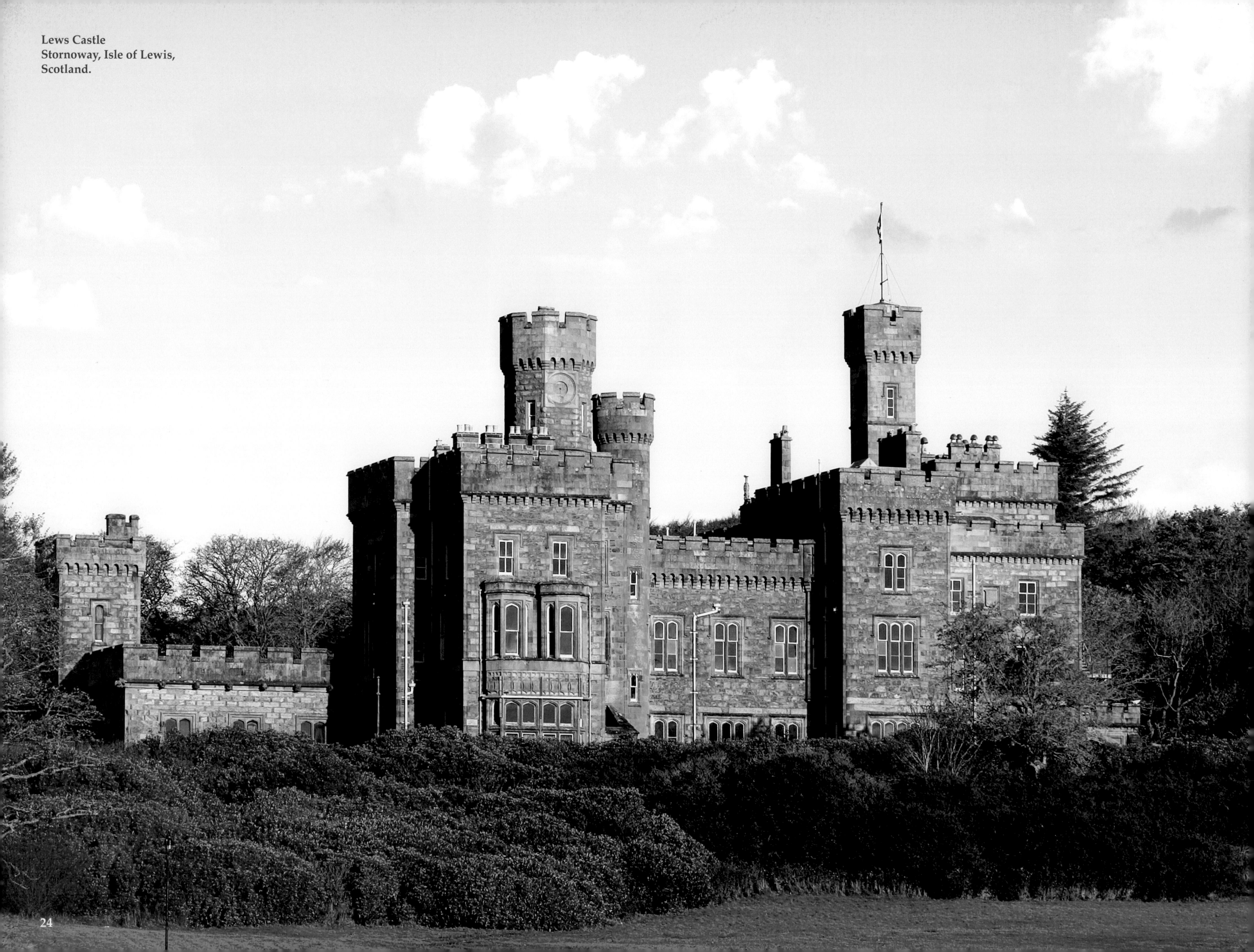

Cardiff Castle, 19th century Victorian Gothic
Revival expansion.

Blarney Castle
Blarney (near Cork), Ireland.

Kylemore Abbey
Connemara, Galway, Ireland.

Belfast Castle
Belfast, Northern Ireland.

Frederiksborg Palace
Hillerød, Denmark.

31

Egeskov Castle,
Funen, Denmark.

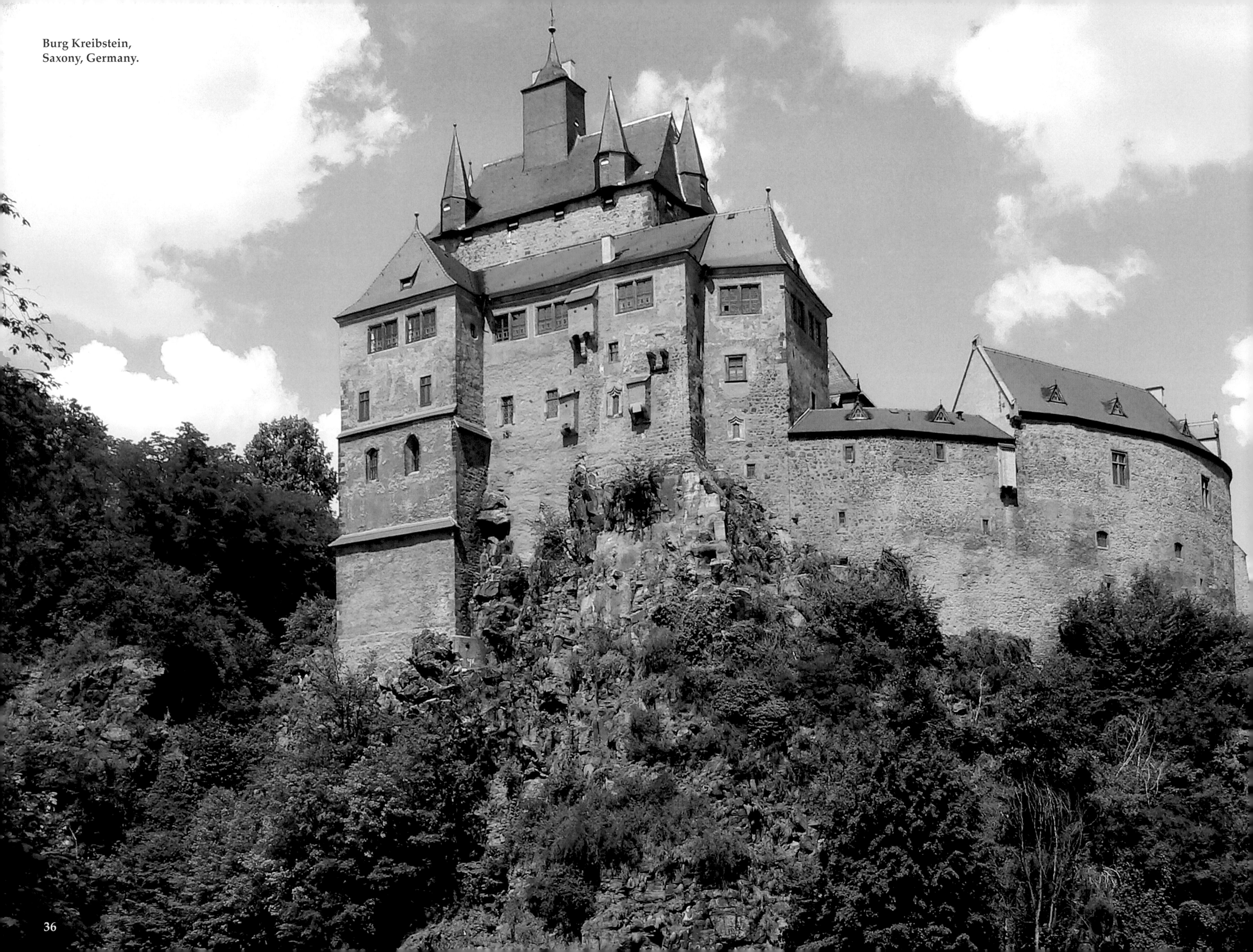

Burg Kreibstein,
Saxony, Germany.

Burg Eltz,
Moselle Valley, Germany.

Burg Thurant,
Moselle Valley, Germany.

38

Schloss Neuschwanstein,
Bavaria, Germany.

39

Burghausen,
Upper Bavaria, Germany.

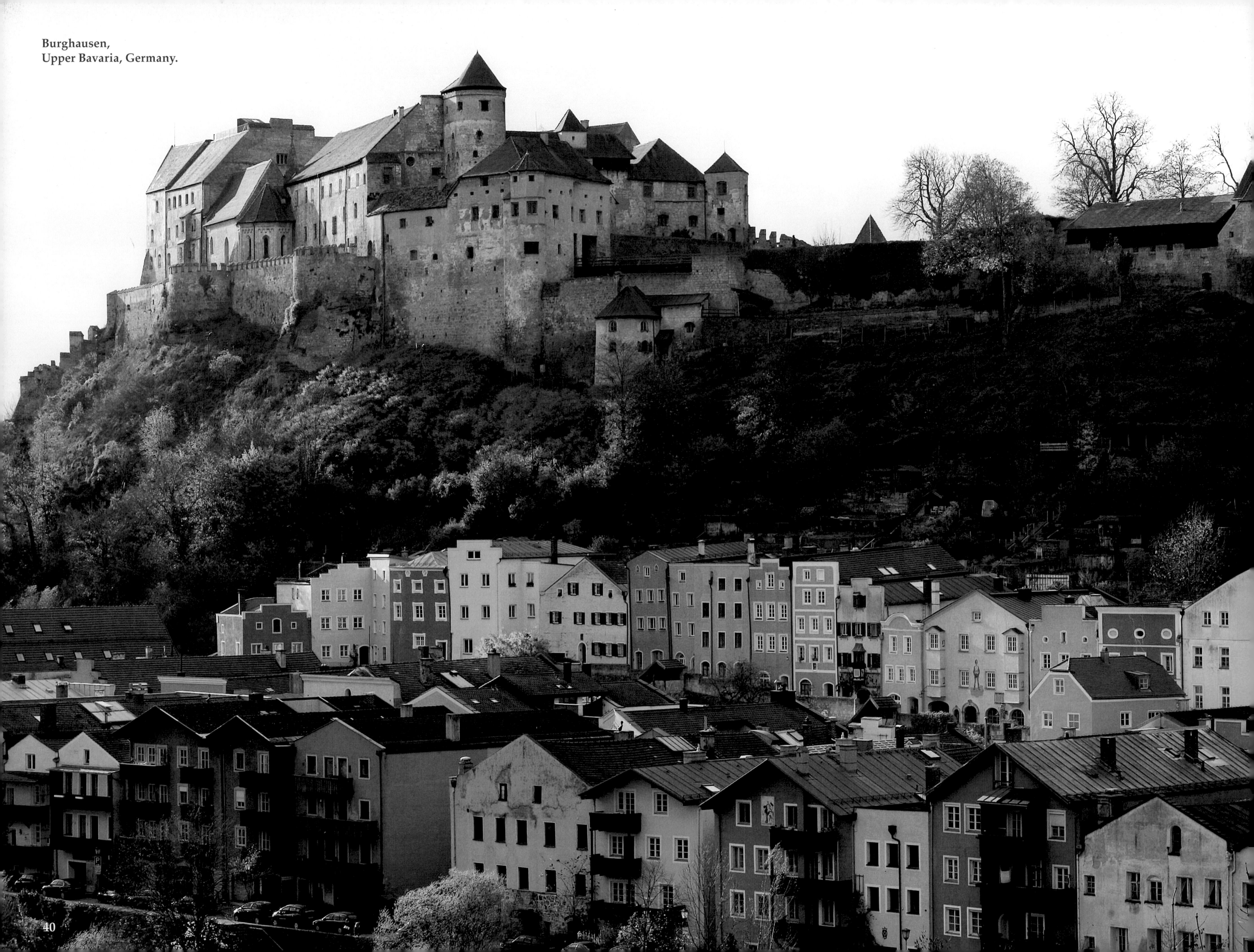

Burg Katz,
St. Goarshausen, Germany.

Burg Hohenwerfen,
Salzburg, Austria.

Vianden Castle,
Vianden, Luxembourg.

Château de Chenonceau,
Loire Valley, France.

45

Cité de Carcassonne,
Aude, France.

Château de Chambord,
Loir-et-Cher, France.

Mont Saint-Michel
Normandy, France.

51

Castle Karlstejn,
Karlstejn, Czech Republic.

53

Bran Castle,
near Brașov, Romania.

Lastochkino Gnezdo,
near Yalta, Ukraine.

Castelo de Óbidos,
Leiria, Portugal.

63

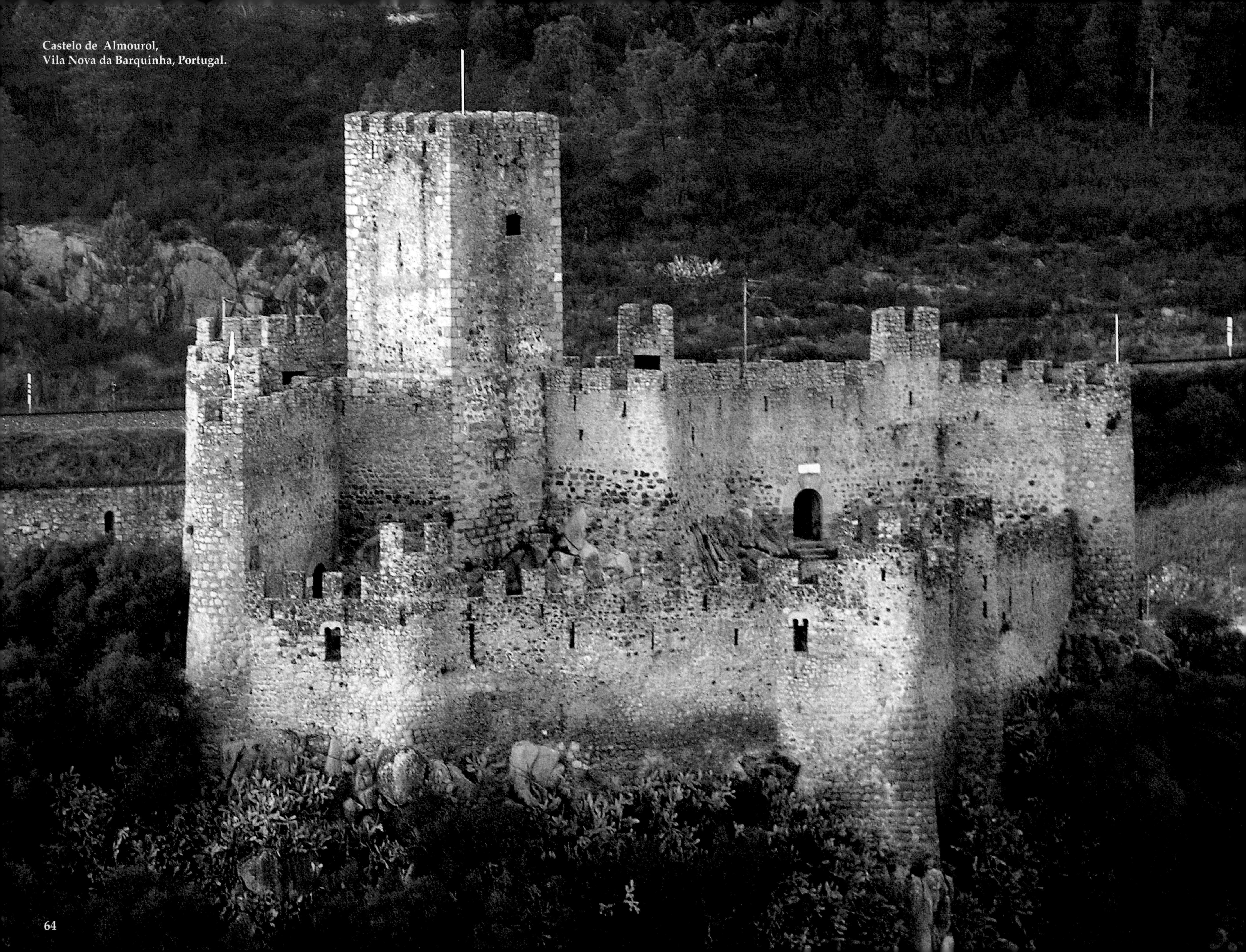

Castelo de Almourol,
Vila Nova da Barquinha, Portugal.

The Alhambra,
Grenada, Spain.

Alcázar de Segovia,
Segovia, Spain.

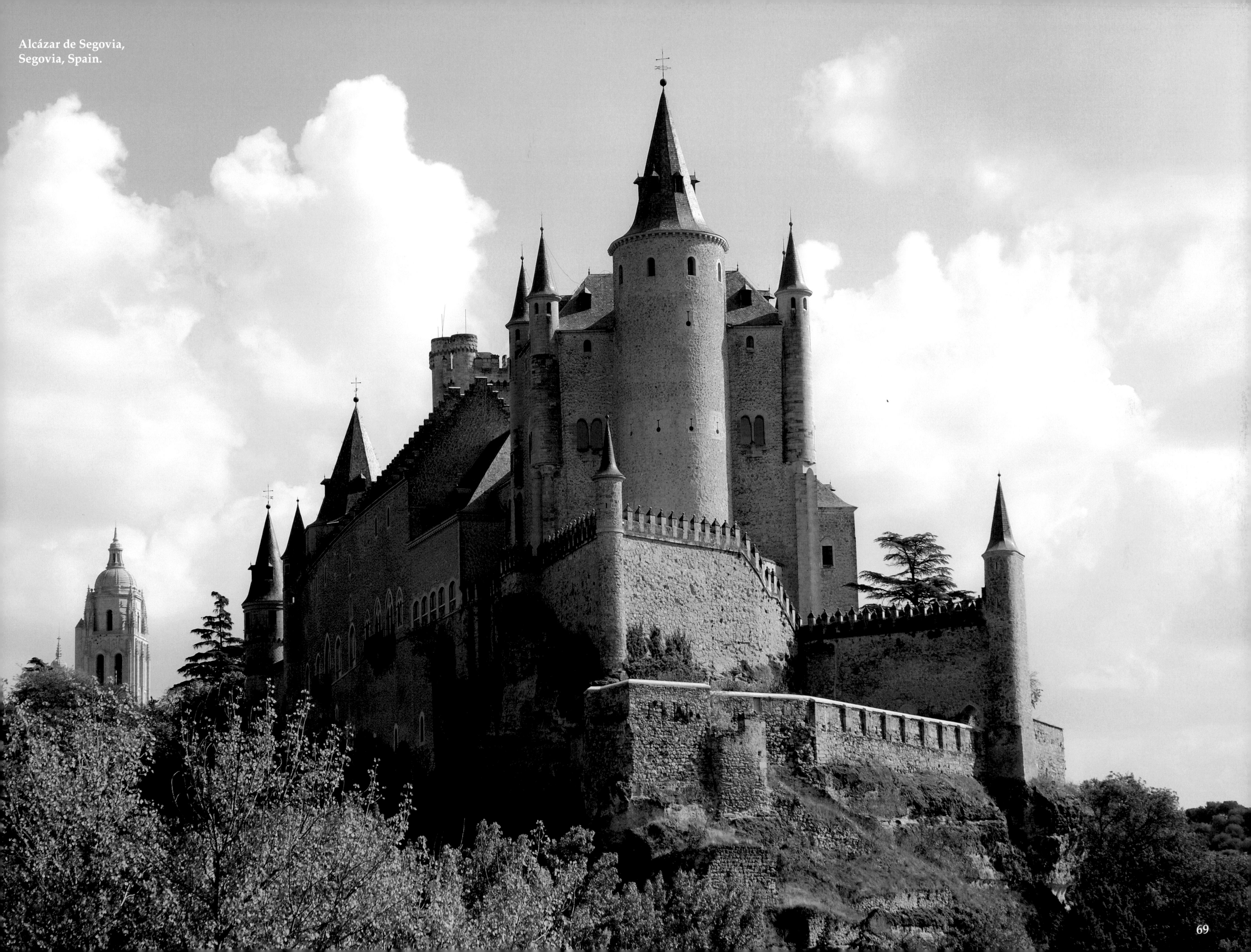

Castle of Saint Pierre,
Aosta Valley, Italy.

Rocca Scaligera,
near Verona, Italy.

VIA
PICCAPOO PRINCEPI
DI CANDIDA GONZACA

Castles ❖ Royal Homes and Fortresses of Europe

Inverary Castle ❖ *page 1*
Strathclyde, Scotland.
1789

This castle is the family seat of the Clan Campbell and the home of the Duke of Argyll. The original design of the castle, incorporating aspects of Baroque, Palladian, and Gothic styles, was begun in 1720 by architect Sir John Vanbrugh. After his death the work was taken over by Roger Morris and William Adam.

Castillo de Belmonte ❖ *pages 2-3*
Belmonte, Castilla La Mancha, Spain.
15th century

The fortress was erected to protect the domain of Juan Pacheco, the Marquis of Villena. Its hexagonally shaped castle embodies a blend of Gothic and Mudéjar architecture, and features a zigzagging wall with cylindrical towers that surrounds a triangular courtyard. It was last occupied in the 19th century.

Castle Conwy (Conway) ❖ *page 4*
in the town of Conwy, Aberconwy, and Colwyn, north Wales.
13th century

It was built in four short years under the supervision of James of St. George for Britain's Edward I after his army had conquered Snowdonia. The castle was constructed to guard the entrance to the River Conway with an outer wall that features eight massive towers over 70 feet high and 90 feet in circumference.

Windsor Castle ❖ *page 5*
Berkshire, England.
11th century

The largest inhabited castle in the world, Windsor was originally a wooden military fortress built by William the Conqueror. His son Henry II was the first sovereign to reside in the castle and built the first stone keep at its center. In the reign of Edward III it began its transformation into the opulent palace we know today.

Bamburgh Castle ❖ *page 6*
Northumberland, England.
11th century

A castle has existed at Bamburgh since the 6th century but the original fortress was destroyed by the Vikings in 993. A new stone castle was constructed by the Normans in the 11th century, was restored by Lord Crewe in the 1750s and more recently by the first Lord Armstrong whose heirs continue to make it their home.

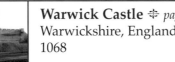

Warwick Castle ❖ *page 7*
Warwickshire, England.
1068

The first castle at Warwick was constructed by William the Conqueror. Over the years it was enlarged and rebuilt in stone, and by the late 14th century Thomas de Beauchamp completed an expansion including the enormous gatehouse and barbican along with two huge towers that command the approaches to the wall.

Caerhays Castle ❖ *page 8*
Cornwall, England.
1810

Designed in the style of a Norman castle by the famed architect John Nash, it was constructed as a country estate for John Bettesworth Trevanion. By 1840 the Trevanions had fallen into debt and fled to Paris abandoning the castle. It was purchased at auction by Michael Willams whose heirs still reside at Caerhays.

Belvoir Castle ❖ *page 9*
Leicestershire, England.
1816

The current castle is the fourth to have stood at this location since Norman times. These castles have been the ancestral home of the Duke of Rutland for over ten centuries. Its current design was executed by the architect John Wyatt under commission from the wife of the 5th Duke. It is now home to the 11th Duke and Duchess.

Bodiam Castle ❖ *page 10*
Sussex, England.
1385

It was built by Sir Edward Dalyngrigge under license from Edward III during the Hundred Years' War to defend the upper River Rother against an expected French invasion. It was owned by a succession of powerful Sussex families until its final restoration by Lord Curzon who bequeathed it to the National Trust in 1926.

Lindisfarne Castle ❖ *page 11*
Holy Island, near Berkwick-upon-Tweed. Northumberland, England.
16th century

The castle was built on Holy Island in the North Sea as a defense against Scottish and Viking attacks. It sits on Beblowe Crag, the highest point on the island, overlooking and protecting Lindisfarne Harbour. Its military importance declined in the reign of James I, who united the Scottish, English and Irish thrones.

Scotney Castle ❖ *page 12*
Lamberhurst, Tunbridge Wells, Kent, England.
14th century

Roger Ashburnham built this fortified country estate around 1380. By the mid-1500s only the south tower remained. In 1580 the south wing was reconstructed and in 1630 the east wing. It was owned by the Darrell family until 1778, then the Hussey family until 1970, when Christopher Hussey left it to the National Trust.

Newark Castle ❖ *page 13*
Nottinghamshire, England.
12th century

A castle on this site was built under Saxon King Egbert in the 9th century but the current structure descends from the one built by Alexander of Lincoln around 1123. A reconstruction was completed in the early 13th century. King John died there in 1216 and it was later used as a prison under Edward III.

The Tower of London ❖ *page 14*
London, England.
1078

Officially, Her Majesty's Royal Palace and Fortress, this castle was built by William the Conqueror in 1078. Throughout its history it has served as a fortress, palace, armory, treasury, mint, and prison, and has been the site of many notable executions. Since 1303, it has housed the Crown Jewels of the United Kingdom.

Hever Castle ❖ *page 15*
Kent, England.
13th century

This castle was the family seat of the Boleyn family and childhood home of Anne Boleyn, the second wife of Henry VIII, who was executed in 1536. After her father died in 1539, the property was held by Henry VIII, and subsequently passed through many hands. It was last renovated by William Waldorf Astor in 1903.

Alnwick Castle ❖ *page 16 & back endleaf*
Northumberland, England.
1096

Alnwick is the second largest inhabited castle in England. It was built by Yves de Vescy, Baron of Alnwick, in 1096 to defend against the Scots. It was owned by the Percys until the early 1400s, and since then by the Earls and Dukes of Northumberland. Current Duke, Ralph George Algernon Percy, resides there today.

Leeds Castle ❖ *page 17*
Kent, England.
1119

This castle was built by Robert de Crevecoeur to replace the earlier Saxon manor of Esledes, which had existed on the site since the 9th century. It was a royal palace of Edward I. Later, Henry VIII spent large sums expanding and beautifying it. Most of the current castle results from 19th century renovations.

Dunrobin Castle ✤ page 18

Southerland, Scotland.
13th century

A castle has stood on this site since the establishment of the Earldom of Southerland in 1235. The early castle keep still exists within the much altered structure we see today. Architect Sir Charles Barry was commissioned in 1845 to remodel the castle in its distinctly french renaissance influenced style.

Balmoral Castle ✤ page 19
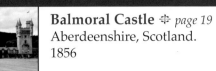
Aberdeenshire, Scotland.
1856

Balmoral is the summer residence of Elizabeth II and the Duke of Edinburgh. In 1390, Sir William Drummond built a home on the site which passed through several owners until it was acquired by Queen Victoria and Price Albert in 1852. Architect William Smith was then commissioned to design and build the castle.

Glamis Castle ✤ page 20
Angus, Scotland.
14th century

Originally built as a hunting lodge for the Earls of Strathmore, it was expanded into a 5-story tower house in the 15th century. In the 17th century it was further expanded to a baronial mansion. It was the childhood home of the Queen Mother; and, in 1930, the birthplace of Princess Margaret.

Palace of Holyroodhouse ✤ page 21

Edinburgh, Scotland.
1128

David I of Scotland built the Augustinian Abbey, on this site in 1128. By the 15th century it was expanded to the royal residence of the Kings and Queens of Scotland. James II was born there in 1430. In 1498 James IV again expanded the palace to it's current grandeur. Elizabeth II uses it when in Scotland for State occasions.

Castle Campbell ✤ page 22

Clackmannanshire, Scotland.
15th century

Originally named Castle Gloom, it was property of the clan Stuart until it passed by marriage to Colin Campbell, 1st Earl of Argyll, who had the name changed in 1489. In the English Civil War, the 8th Earl sided with Cromwell against the King. In retaliation the Scots burned the castle in 1654 ending its use as a residence.

Caerlaverock Castle ✤ page 23

Southeast of Dumfries, Scotland.
13th century

The only triangular castle in the United Kingdom, it was built by the Maxwells to defend Scotland against attacks by Edward I. It fell to the English in a siege in 1300 and remained in their hands for 12 years. The castle was dismantled by 1357, and was rebuilt in the 15th century, only to be partially dismantled again in 1640.

Lews Castle ✤ page 24
Stornoway, Isle of Lewis, Scotland.
1857

This Victorian era castle was built as a country estate for Sir James Matheson who had made his fortune in the opium trade. In 1918 it was purchased by industrialist Lord Leverhulme who gave it to the people of Stornoway in 1923. During World War II it housed the 700 Naval Air Squadron who operated from the island.

Edinburgh Castle ✤ page 25

Edinburgh, Scotland.
12th century

This ancient fortress sits upon Castle Rock overlooking the city of Edinburgh. Its oldest structure, St. Margaret's Chapel, dates back to the early 12th century. The first meeting of the Scottish Parliament was held at the castle around 1140. During the reign of David I Edinburgh grew as a site of royal power.

Cardiff Castle ✤ page 26

Cardiff, Wales.
11th century

The Norman keep was constructed about 1091 by Robert Fitzhamon, Lord of Gloucester and conqueror of Glamorgan. In the early 19th century the castle was expanded in the Gothic Revival style, and in 1898 work was begun on a massive expansion to create a romantic castle in the Victorian Gothic Revival style.

Blarney Castle ✤ page 27
Blarney (near Cork), Ireland.
1446

Legend has it that Robert the Bruce gave Cormac Mc-Carthy half of the storied Stone of Scone. When the third castle on this site was later erected by Dermot McCarthy, King of Munster, it was incorporated into the battlements where it is now known as the Blarney Stone. Kissing it is thought to bestow the gift of eloquence.

Kylemore Abbey ✤ page 28

Connemara, Galway, Ireland.
1868

This neo-gothic castle was built by Michell Henry in memory of his late wife Margaret. Its most famous feature is the miniature cathedral that serves as its chapel. Since 1920 it has been home to the Irish Benedictine nuns who established a school there that is still operating today.

Belfast Castle ✤ page 29
Belfast, Northern Ireland.
1870

Castles have existed on this site since the late 12th century. The current castle was designed in the Scottish baronial style by Charles Lanyon and his son for the 3rd Marquis of Donegall. It later came in to the possession of the 8th Earl of Shaftesbury whose son gave the castle to the city of Belfast in 1934.

Olavinlinna ✤ page 30

Savonlinna, Finland.
15th century

Its name translates as St. Olaf's Castle. Its location lies further north than any other medieval castle still standing. The fortress was built by a Danish knight, Erik Axelsson Tott, to defend the province of Savonia from Russian attack. Its military importance continued and there was a garrison stationed there until 1847.

Frederiksborg Palace ✤ page 31
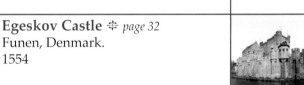
Hillerød, Denmark.
1560

The original castle was built by Frederick II after whom it is named, but it was largely revised from 1602 to 1620 by Christian IV using Dutch architects, Hans and Lorents van Steenwinckel. Christian IV used it as his royal residence until his death in 1648, after which it was mainly used for ceremonial events.

Egeskov Castle ✤ page 32
Funen, Denmark.
1554

It was built by Frands Brockenhuus as a fortified home shortly after a period of general civil unrest in Denmark. It is built over a shallow lake on a foundation of oak pilings. Legend has it that an entire oak forest was felled to construct its base, hence the name Egeskov which translates as "oak forest."

Gravensteen Castle ✤ page 33
Ghent, Belgium.
1180

Count Philip of Alsace modeled his castle after the crusaders' castles that he had seen during his participation in the second crusade. Gravensteen served as the seat of the Counts of Flanders until the 14th century and later served as a courthouse and prison. It was restored by the city of Ghent in 1885.

Het Steen ✤ page 34

Antwerp, Belgium.
1225

Het Steen is the oldest building in Antwerp. Its location commanded control of the river Schelde that flows through Antwerp. It was significantly modified by Charles V around 1520. It also served as a prison from 1303 to 1827.

Muiderslot ✤ page 35
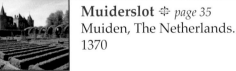
Muiden, The Netherlands.
1370

In 1280, Count Floris V built a stone castle at this location in order to collect a toll from traders traveling the River Vecht to Ultrecht. Although that castle did not survive, one hundred years later, Albrecht, Duke of Bavaria, rebuilt it according to the original plans. The beautiful gardens were added in the 17th century.

Burg Kriebstein ✤ page 36

Saxony, Germany.
14th century

Towering above the River Mulde on a steep rock outcropping this castle is one of the best preserved examples of Late Gothic construction in all of Saxony. It was originally built for Earl Wilhelm I of Meissen, and was subsequently substantially modified by the succeeding owner, Hugold of Schleinitz.

Burg Eltz ✤ page 37 & front cover
Moselle Valley, Germany.
12th century

This medieval castle sits in the hills overlooking the Moselle valley. It is surrounded on three sides by the Elzbach River, a tributary on the north side of the Moselle. Construction of various additions continued into the 16th century. Burg Eltz is a Ganerbenburg—that is, it belongs to a community of joint heirs.

Burg Thurant ❖ *page 38*
Moselle Valley, Germany.
1197

This castle was built by Heinrich, a brother of King Otto IV. In the mid-13th century it came, by treaty, into the possession of two Archbishops, Arnold II of Trier and Konrad von Hochstaden of Cologne, who divided the castle between them. Each half has its own separate entrance, residence, and dungeon.

Schloss Neuschwanstein ❖ *page 39*
Bavaria, Germany.
19th century

This castle was built by Ludwig II as a mountain retreat and homage to composer Richard Wagner. The interior is decorated with scenes from Wagnerian operas. Its whimsical design is thought to have been the inspiration for the Sleeping Beauty Castle in Disneyland.

Burghausen ❖ *page 40*
Upper Bavaria, Germany.
6th century

At 1,043 meters (3422 feet—almost ⅔ mi.), this is the longest castle in Europe. It is thought to have been constructed between the 6th and 8th centuries to collect tolls on the Salzach River. It continued to be extended until the 16th century when it reached its current length.

Burg Katz ❖ *page 41*
St. Goarshausen, Germany.
1371

It was originally constructed as a military base by Count Wilhelm II of Katzenelnbogen on a rocky ledge overlooking the Rhine. This commanding position was also used to collect tolls from merchants on the river. It was destroyed by Napoleon in 1806 during French occupation but was rebuilt between 1896 and 1898.

Burg Hohenwerfen ❖ *page 42*
Salzburg, Austria.
11th century

This majestic alpine fortress served the rulers of Salzburg as a military base, residence, and hunting retreat. It was expanded during the 12th century and again during the 16th. It has also seen duty as a state prison housing numerous high-ranking noblemen over the course of its history,

Vianden Castle ❖ *page 43*
Vianden, Luxembourg.
11th century

The castle was built over the course of the 11th through 14th centuries and served as the seat of power for the Counts of Vianden. While it underwent continued development into the 18th century, it fell into disrepair after the departure of the Counts of Luxembourg. Under state ownership it has recently been restored.

Château de Saumur ❖ *page 44*
Loire Valley, France.
10th century

It was originally built by Thibault le Tricheur, comte de Blois, to defend against Norman attacks. In the early 13th century it was part of the royal domain of Philip II. Passing through numerous owners, it was later used as a prison under Napoleon's rule. In the 20th century it was acquired and restored by the city of Saumur.

Château de Chenonceau ❖ *page 45*
Loire Valley, France.
1515

Construction of this château was begun by Thomas Bohier, Chamberlain for Charles VIII, and completed by his wife Katherine Briçonnet. François I seized it from Bohier's son for unpaid debts to the Crown. It was saved from destruction in the French Revolution by its function as an important bridge over the River Cher.

Château de Chantilly ❖ *page 46*
Chantilly, France.
16th century

It is made up of two attached buildings. The original Grand Château, built in 1528–1531 for the Constable Anne de Montmorency, was destroyed in the French Revolution and rebuilt in the 1870s. The Petite Château was added around 1560. Moliere's play, *Les Précieuses ridicules*, was first performed here in 1659.

Château d'Azay-le-Rideau ❖ *page 47*
Chinon, France.
1068

Gilles Berthelot, state treasurer of François I and mayor of Tours, built this château on an island in the Indre River. In 1528, Berthelot fled under suspicion of embezzlement and the estate was seized by the crown. It changed hands numerous times until the early 20th century when it was restored by the French government.

Cité de Carcassonne ❖ *pages 48–49*
Aude, France.
1st century BC

Originally fortified by the Romans around 100BC. Additional Fortifications were added by the Visigoth king Theodoric II who took possession in 453. Saracens from Barcelona captured it in 725 but were driven out by Pippin the Younger in 759. The fortress was thoroughly restored in 1853 by architect Eugène Viollet-le-Duc.

Château de Chambord ❖ *page 50*
Loir-et-Cher, France.
1547

Thought to have been built by François I primarily as a hunting lodge but also to be near to his mistress the Comtesse de Thoury, it is the largest castle in the Loire Valley. This castle incorporates a central keep with bastion towers at its corners; however, its fortifications, moat and towers are purely decorative in nature.

Mont Saint-Michel ❖ *page 51*
Normandy, France.
8th century

Although a Romano-Breton stronghold since the 6th century, the monastery that forms the basis for subsequent fortifications was constructed in the 8th century. Over the years it was strengthened and able to withstand numerous assaults by the English during the Hundred Years' War. It was restored in the 19th century.

Reszel Castle ❖ *page 52*
Reszel, Poland.
1401

This castle was built on the bank of the River Sajna by the Teutonic Order, a German Roman Catholic religious order. They used it in their efforts to maintain control of the region, which they had captured from its Prussian founders. In 1410 a Polish-Lithuanian army defeated the order and broke its military hold.

Castle Karlstejn ❖ *page 53*
Karlstejn, Czech Republic.
1365

This castle was constructed by the Holy Roman Emperor Charles IV. The Chapel of the Holy Cross, located in the Great Tower, was consecrated in 1365. This fortress was home to the Czech crown jewels for almost 200 years. Its most recent major renovation was completed in 1899 by architect Josef Mocker.

Fisherman's Bastion ❖ *page 54*
Budapest, Hungary.
1902

This terrace, combining neo-Romanesque and neo-Gothic styles, was built on the Castle Hill on the Buda bank of the Danube. Its seven towers symbolize the seven Magyar tribes that settled in the Carpathian Basin. It occupies the site of the medieval ramparts once used to defend this area of the city.

Veliki Tabor Castle ❖ *page 55*
near Desinića, Zagorje, Croatia.
12th century

The oldest portion of the castle, the Five-Cornered Tower, was built in the 12th century. Additional towers were completed in the 15th and 16th centuries. A chapel on the first floor contains the skull of Veronika of Desinić, whose ghost is said to haunt the castle with her screams in the night.

Bran Castle ❖ *page 56*
near Brașov, Romania.
14th century

Also known as Dracula's Castle, it was built to defend against attacks by the Ottoman Empire. Though it seems never to have been the residence of Vlad Țepeș (Dracula, Vlad the Impaler), records indicate that he may have briefly been held prisoner here during the Ottoman occupation of Transylvania.

Predjama Castle ❖ *page 57*
Predjama, Slovenia.
1274

Built by the Aquileian patriarchs in Gothic style, this castle is sheltered by a natural rocky arch high on a cliff wall making access to it extremely difficult. A secret natural shaft leads from the castle into the Postojnska cave system allowing it to be covertly restocked with food and supplies during times of siege.

Pskov Kremlin ❖ *page 58*
Pskov, Russia.
12th century

The Krom (fortress) was built on a long rocky ridge between the Velikaya and Pskova Rivers beginning with the construction of the cathedral and Spaso-Mirozhskiy monastery. Fortified walls and towers were added in the 13th century. Pskov was fought over by the Russians, Germans, and Lithuanians during that period.

The Kremlin ⁜ *page 59*
Moscow, Russia.
14th century

This site has been inhabited since the 2nd millennium BC. The first stone structures were built in the reign of Ivan I, and Prince Dmitri Donskoi added limestone walls in 1368. They are incorporated in the current walls and towers, which were completed by Italian masters in 1495. Numerous buildings have been added since.

Khotyn Fortress ⁜ *page 60*
Khotyn, Ukraine.
13th century

A fort was built here on the shores of the Dniester River in the 10th century by Prince Vladimir Svyatoslavich to defend the border of Kievan Rus'. King Daniel of Galicia and his son Lev ordered a rebuilding in 1264. In the late 1300s, under Stephen the Great of Moldavia, the fortress was expanded to its current form.

Lastochkino Gnezdo ⁜ *page 61*
near Yalta, Ukraine.
1912

This castle's name translates as the "Swallow's Nest." It was designed by architect Leonid Sherwood and built on Aurora Cliff overlooking Ai–Todor cape on the Black Sea. Baron von Steinheil, a Baltic German noble who had made a fortune extracting oil in Baku, commissioned the structure as a residence.

Castelo de Guimarães ⁜ *page 62*
Braga, Minho, Portugal.
10th century

Dona Mumadona Dias ordered this castle built to defend Guimarães' monastery from Muslim and Norman attacks. It was extensively renovated and expanded in the 11th century when Count Dom Henrique chose to locate his royal court here. It continued as a royal residence through much of the 12th century.

Castelo de Óbidos ⁜ *page 63*
Leiria, Portugal.
12th century

An ancient Roman castle stood on this ground, but when the area was conquered from the Moors in 1148 the castle began to evolve into the Manueline-style structure we see today. In the 13th century King Dinis presented it as a gift to his wife, Queen Isabel de Aragon. In 1755, serious earthquake damage was repaired.

Castelo de Almourol ⁜ *page 64*
Vila Nova da Barquinha, Portugal.
12th century

This fortress is located on a small rocky island in the middle of the Tagus River. It was constructed by the Knights Templar on the site of an ancient Roman fortification. It had military importance in defending the capital of Portugal, then Coimbra, from Moorish attacks during the Portugese *Reconquista.*

Torre de Belém ⁜ *page 65*
Lisbon, Portugal.
16th century

The tower was built under the authority of Juan II as part of the defense system for the mouth of the Tagus River and also served as a ceremonial gateway to the city of Lisbon. It was designed and constructed by military architect, Francisco de Arruda. King Ferdinand II had it restored and embellished in the 1840s.

The Alhambra ⁜ *page 66*
Grenada, Spain.
14th century

This beautiful palace and fortress was constructed as the residence for the Moorish monarchs of Grenada. Its full name "Qal'at al-Hambra" translates as "the red fortress," and derives from the red clay of the surrounding area. In 1492, it fell to the Christians in an attack by the forces of Ferdinand II of Aragon.

Castillo de Manzanares el Real ⁜ *page 67*
near Madrid, Spain.
15th century

Construction of this Gothic and Mudejar influnced castle commenced in 1475 under the auspices of the powerful Mendoza family. Title over Manzaneres de Real was granted to the family in 1445 by Juan II for their military support. All of the lower barbican walls have arrow loops in the shape of the cross of Jerusalem.

Castillo de Turégano ⁜ *page 68*
near Segovia, Spain.
15th century

This medieval castle was built by Juan Arias Dávila, the Archbisop of Saville, who had decided to make Turégano into his personal fortress. The castle was built to surround the Church of San Miguel, which dates to the late 12th or early 13th century. In 1585, Antonio Perez, secretary of King Philip II, was imprisoned here.

Alcázar de Segovia ⁜ *page 69*
Segovia, Spain.
12th century

This castle was built over the ruins of an ancient Roman fortress. During the middle ages it was one of the favorite royal residences of the Kings of Castille. It was continuously modified until the 16th century when the conical towers were added. Throughout the 17th and 18th centuries it was used as a prison.

Castle of Saint Pierre ⁜ *page 70*
Aosta Valley, Italy.
12th century

The earliest recorded owners were the brothers de castro Sancti Petri. In the 17th century Pietro Filiberto Roncas enlarged and redesigned the castle to its current form. The French-influenced conical roofs on its four lateral towers lend this castle an almost fairytale quality as it sits high on a rocky crag in the Italian Alps.

Castello de Guaita ⁜ *page 71*
San Marino, Italy.
11th century

The First Tower, or *Rocca*, is the oldest of three towers constructed on the peaks of Monte Titano to defend the city of San Marino. In the 13th century it was modified under the supevision of the Comacine Masters, famed stonemasons of the period, and subsequent additional alterations were made in the 15th and 16th centuries.

Rocca Scaligera ⁜ *page 72*
Sirmione, near Verona, Italy.
13th century

Also known as Sirmione Castle, this opulent fortified home was built largely as a show of wealth by the prominent Della Scalla family of Verona. It occupies the tip of a 2½ mile long spit of land that juts out into Lake Garda. After its construction it became the base for the family's fleet of warships used to patrol their holdings.

Castel Nuovo ⁜ *page 73*
Naples, Italy.
13th century

This fortress was built by order of Charles I of Anjou, and was originally named the Maschio Angioino (the Angevin Keep). Following his victory over the French, Alfonso of Aragon commissioned an extensive renovation that expanded and fortified the structure, which was then renamed Castel Nuovo (New Castle).

Castel Sant'Angelo ⁜ *page 74*
Rome, Italy.
2nd century

Originally the tomb of the Roman Emperor Hadrian, this structure has been extensively modified over centuries of use. It was converted into a fortress in 401, and later into a castle in the 14th century by Pope Nicholas III. Its name stems from a legend that the Archangel Michael appeared here at the end of the plague of 590.

Castle of Bourtzi ⁜ *page 75*
Nafplio, Greece.
15th century

This island fortress was built by the Venetians to protect the harbor city of Nafplio from pirates and naval attacks. It continued to serve as a fortress under various rulers including the Turks and Greeks until 1865 when it was converted to a residence for the executioners of prisoners at the Fortress of Palamidi.

Château de Chillon ⁜ *front endleaf*
Lake Geneva, Switzerland.
12th century

Built on a site that has been occupied since the Bronze Age, this castle was originally used by the House of Savoy to control the trade route along the shores of Lake Geneva. It was captured by the Bernese Swiss in 1536 who held the fortress until the Vaudois Revolution in 1798. It became property of the Canton of Vaud in 1803.

Photography Credits

Jacket front: Image © 2007 by ultimathule. Used under license from Shutterstock.com

Front endleaf: Image © 2007 by kavram. Used under license from Shutterstock.com

Back endleaf: Image © 2007 by Darren Turner. Used under license from Shutterstock.com

Page 1: Image © 2007 by Andrey Kozachenko. Used under license from Shutterstock.com

Pages 2–3: Image © 2007 by Matt Trommer. Used under license from Shutterstock.com

Page 4: Image © 2007 by Kevin Crumplin. Used under license from Shutterstock.com

Page 5: Main image © 2007 by Hazeelin Hassan. Used under license from Shutterstock.com

Left inset image © 2007 by Margaret Smeaton. Used under license from Shutterstock.com

Right inset image © 2007 by Stephen Mulcahey. Used under license from Shutterstock.com

Page 6: Image © 2007 by Steve Smith. Used under license from Shutterstock.com

Page 7: Main image © 2007 by Vladimir Korostyshevskiy. Used under license from Shutterstock.com

Inset image © 2007 by Chad Bontrager. Used under license from Shutterstock.com

Page 8: Image © 2007 by Kevin Britland. Used under license from Shutterstock.com

Page 9: Image © 2007 by Ian Bracegirdle. Used under license from Shutterstock.com

Page 10: Image © 2007 by Graham Taylor. Used under license from Shutterstock.com

Page 11: Image © 2007 by Andrew Barker. Used under license from Shutterstock.com

Page 12: Image © 2007. Used under license from Shutterstock.com

Page 13: Image © 2007 by Ingvar Tjostheim. Used under license from Shutterstock.com

Page 14: Main image © Geoffrey Hammond. Used under license from IStockPhoto.com

Inset image © 2007 by Vladimir Korostyshevskiy. Used under license from Shutterstock.com

Page 15: Image © 2007 by Cabot Harrington. Used under license from Shutterstock.com

Page 16: Image © 2007 by Darren Turner. Used under license from Shutterstock.com

Page 17: Main image © 2007 by MARKABOND. Used under license from Shutterstock.com

Inset image © 2007 by Olga Solovei. Used under license from Shutterstock.com

Page 18: Image © 2007 by Stephen Beaumont. Used under license from Shutterstock.com

Page 19: Image © 2007 by Richard Kittenberger. Used under license from IStockPhoto.com

Page 20: Image © 2007 by Terry Kettlewell. Used under license from Shutterstock.com

Page 21: Main image © 2007 by Bill McKelvie. Used under license from Shutterstock.com

Inset image © 2007 by Ai-Lan Lee. Used under license from Shutterstock.com

Page 22: Image © 2007 by Bill McKelvie. Used under license from Shutterstock.com

Page 23: Image © 2007 by Roger Pilkington. Used under license from Shutterstock.com

Page 24: Image © 2007 by Bill McKelvie. Used under license from Shutterstock.com

Page 25: Image © 2007 by Bill McKelvie. Used under license from Shutterstock.com

Page 26: Main image © 2007 by Rainbow. Used under license from Shutterstock.com

Inset image: Photomechanical print published between ca. 1890 and ca. 1900, Detroit Publishing Co. From the collections of the Library of Congress.

Page 27: Image © 2007 by L Kelly. Used under license from Shutterstock.com

Page 28: Image © 2007 by Mary E. Cioffi. Used under license from Shutterstock.com

Page 29: Image © 2007 by Joy Brown. Used under license from Shutterstock.com

Page 30: Image © 2007 by Tatiana Edrenkina. Used under license from Shutterstock.com

Page 31: Image © 2007 by Irina Korshunova. Used under license from Shutterstock.com

Page 32: Image © 2007 by Willem Dijkstra. Used under license from Shutterstock.com

Page 33: Image © 2007 by Anyka. Used under license from Shutterstock.com

Page 34: Image © 2007 by Jason Merideth. Used under license from Shutterstock.com

Page 35: Image © 2007 by E.G.Pors. Used under license from Shutterstock.com

Page 36: Image © 2007 by Nikita Tiunov. Used under license from Shutterstock.com

Page 37: Image © 2007 by 0293285137. Used under license from Shutterstock.com

Page 38: Image © 2007 by Philip Lange. Used under license from Shutterstock.com

Page 39: Main image © 2007 by Maugli. Used under license from Shutterstock.com

Inset image: Photomechanical print published between ca. 1890 and ca. 1900, Detroit Publishing Co. From the collections of the Library of Congress.

Page 40: Image © 2007 by Rene Grothmann. Used under license from Shutterstock.com

Page 41: Image © 2007 by Iryna Shpulak. Used under license from Shutterstock.com

Page 42: Image © 2007 by Joerg Humpe. Used under license from Shutterstock.com

Page 43: Image © 2007 by Gerrit. Used under license from Shutterstock.com

Page 44: Image © 2007 by Jan van der Hoeven. Used under license from Shutterstock.com

Page 45: Main image © 2007 by Dvoretskiy Igor Vladimirovich. Used under license from Shutterstock.com

Inset image © 2007 by Demid. Used under license from Shutterstock.com

Page 46: Image © 2007 by David Hughes. Used under license from Shutterstock.com

Page 47: Image © 2007 by Alexander Shargin. Used under license from Shutterstock.com

Pages 48-49: Image © 2007 by Lagui. Used under license from Shutterstock.com

Page 49: Inset image © 2007 by Mikhail Lavrenov. Used under license from Shutterstock.com

Page 50: Image © 2007 by Bart Parren. Used under license from Shutterstock.com

Page 51: Image © 2007 by Cristina CIOCHINA. Used under license from Shutterstock.com

Page 52: Image © 2007 by puchan. Used under license from Shutterstock.com

Page 53: Image © 2007 by Rostislav Glinsky. Used under license from Shutterstock.com

Page 54: Image © 2007 by Lazar Mihai-Bogdan. Used under license from Shutterstock.com

Page 55: Image © 2007 by ahkim. Used under license from Shutterstock.com

Page 56: Image © 2007 by Ioan Nicolae. Used under license from Shutterstock.com

Page 57: Image © 2007 by Tomislav Stajduhar. Used under license from Shutterstock.com

Page 58: Image © 2007 by Alexander Avdeev. Used under license from Shutterstock.com

Page 59: Image © 2007 by Michael Mihin. Used under license from Shutterstock.com

Page 60: Image © 2007 by Mostovyi Sergii Igorevich. Used under license from Shutterstock.com

Page 61: Image © 2007 by Lukin Dmitry. Used under license from Shutterstock.com

Page 62: Image © 2007. Used under license from Shutterstock.com

Page 63: Image © 2007 by Antonio Jorge Nunes. Used under license from Shutterstock.com

Page 64: Image © 2007 by Rui Vale de Sousa. Used under license from Shutterstock.com

Page 65: Image © 2007 by Bruno Medley. Used under license from Shutterstock.com

Page 66: Main image © 2007 by Camilo Torres. Used under license from Shutterstock.com

Left inset image © 2007 by Nick Stubbs. Used under license from Shutterstock.com

Right inset image © 2007 by Jennifer Stone. Used under license from Shutterstock.com

Page 67: Image © 2007 by Elena Aliaga. Used under license from Shutterstock.com

Page 68: Image © 2007 by Matt Trommer. Used under license from Shutterstock.com

Page 69: Image © 2007 by Philip Lange. Used under license from Shutterstock.com

Page 70: Image © 2007 by Gertjan Hooijer. Used under license from Shutterstock.com

Page 71: Image © 2007 by Mikhail Nekrasov. Used under license from Shutterstock.com

Page 72: Main and inset images © 2007 by Khirman Vladimir. Used under license from Shutterstock.com

Page 73: Image © 2007 by Cornel Achirei. Used under license from Shutterstock.com

Page 74: Image © 2007 by ultimathule. Used under license from Shutterstock.com

Page 75: Image © 2007 by Nikita Rogul. Used under license from Shutterstock.com